Northern Lights

Written by Suzy Senior

Illustrated by Andrew Pagram

Collins

a crowd troops up a steep hill

a scarf trails in the wind

a crowd troops up a steep hill

a scarf trails in the wind

owls swoop from the trees

bats swoosh in the darkness

owls swoop from the trees

bats swoosh in the darkness

children look up and point

twisting trails of light

children look up and point

twisting trails of light

stunning bright smears of green and pink

the crowd stands still

stunning bright smears of green and pink

the crowd stands still

a person snaps the northern lights

a clear sight on the tablet

a person snaps the northern lights

a clear sight on the tablet

Review: After reading

Use your assessment from hearing the children read to choose any GPCs, words or tricky words that need additional practice.

Read 1: Decoding
- Turn to pages 6 and 7. Point to **darkness** and show the children how to read each chunk of the word (*dark/ness*) and then read the whole word. Support the children to chunk and read the following words in the same way:

  children (*child/ren*) **twisting** (*twist/ing*)

  person (*per/son*) **northern** (*north/ern*)

  Say: Can you blend in your head when you read these words aloud?
- Ask the children to read pages 18 and 19, checking that they don't miss sounding out any of the consonants.

Read 2: Vocabulary
- Look back through the book and discuss the pictures. Encourage the children to talk about details that stand out for them. Use a dialogic talk model to expand on their ideas and recast them in full sentences as naturally as possible.
- Work together to expand vocabulary by naming objects in the pictures that children do not know.
- On page 11, discuss the meaning of **twisting** and **trails**. Say: In the book twisting means that the light goes round in spirals. The lights twist in the sky. They leave trails of light. Trails are paths. Discuss other things that can make a twisting trail of light. (e.g. *sparklers*)

Read 3: Comprehension
- Ask the children whether they have ever gone out at night and seen stars, or the moon, or fireworks. How did they feel when they saw these things?
- Reread pages 2 and 3 and discuss why lots of people might be gathering in a crowd. Talk about how the northern lights are a rare thing to see.
- Use the pictures on pages 22 and 23 to model how to recap the content of the book. Ask the children to have a go.